FRACTURED MIRROR

GRIEVING BEAUTIFULLY IMPERFECT: A JOURNEY THROUGH THE FIRST YEAR OF GRIEF

MARK TRIBOULET

Poems and Prose

Fractured Mirror Grieving Beautifully Imperfect: A Journey Through the First Year of Grief
Copyright © 2026 Mark Triboulet
Published by Speak Fire Publishing: www.speakfire.today

All rights reserved. No portion of this book may be reproduced or transmitted in any form or by any means, electronic or mechanical, without the express written permission from Mark Triboulet except as permitted by U.S. copyright law.

Request for permission to make copies of any part of this work should be directed to mtriboulet@socalsem.edu

ISBNs:
Print: 978-1-958978-39-9
eBook 978-1-958978-40-5
Hardback 978-1-958978-41-2

Manufactured in the United States of America

Library of Congress Control Number: 2026903709

Cover Design: Sharon Marta
Chapter Header Image: Sharon Marta

Live like Laurie sticker designed by Mary Stuart Gorsuch

Advance Praise

Kollen Kennedy: Resounding Praise Hand Bell Choir Director, and Laurie's dear friend

Honestly, I loved it all! I blubbered my way through it and had to put it aside often in order to digest my emotions and thoughts. All I have felt and "pictured" in these last almost five years are in these pages. Mark's writing is so relatable. I felt every fear, question, frustration...every ounce of anger, confusion, depression and yet...the weight of hope can cut through all of that to reach us!

So real. Seeking answers.

Love the ocean imagery...also made me think of Laurie's beautiful eyes. How I miss her!!

We always talk about the "big events" people gone will miss...but it's the "new normal" of everyday moments that slams ya in the gut.

Mark shows how hyper all our senses become...internally and externally. How important his writings are...for those especially that don't know how to put into words This! Exact! Thought!

Jennifer (Jen) Peterson: Resounding Praise Hand Bell Choir Director, and Laurie's dear friend

Grief...soul sucking, gut wrenching, all-consuming, infinite yet temporary. On an early morning in February my dear friend slipped into the arms of Christ and out of my earthly life, leaving grief in her wake. She was finally at full peace at the end of her journey and mine was just beginning. Mark was her rock, her love, her soulmate and is, to this day, my friend. His heart shows in this book the pain of grief, allowing the reader to relate it to their own.

The vivid paintings conjured by his writing show the reality of life without your loved one by your side. Seeing the stages of grief written down allows me to relate to its ups and downs and know that they are normal and healthy. Grieving is a process that cannot be rushed or shoved aside.
Mark's poetry put into words what I could not. I embarked on his journey in these pages only to see my own journey reflected.

Shameless, raw, heartfelt and depicting the hope and strength that comes through taking the journey wherever it leads. Feel the pain, cry the tears, survive the dark nights and experience the sun peeking out at the start of a new journey.

Dedication

In loving memory of Laurel (Laurie) Lynn Triboulet
11-12-72 to 2-22-21

I have no words.
And yet, I wrote a book of my grief for you.
How is any number of words enough?
How many books does it take to describe how much I loved and still love you?
May you be honored by what is written here.
May your legacy be lived out by those who knew you and loved you.

Table of Contents

INTRODUCTION

I started writing this book, not as a book, but as a way to vent and cope with my own thoughts, feelings, and grief.

It was all I could do. I gave myself permission to write exactly what I felt. Right or wrong, I wrote.

At some point, I realized just how much and often people stuff their feelings inside and avoid their own grief, dragging unprocessed things around with them like a bag of rocks. As I attempted to unload my own bag of rocks, I questioned and was questioned about the way I unpacked them. I was told I was not doing it right or that I had to do it "this way" or "that way," which frustrated me. And all I wanted was permission to feel whatever it was I felt, right or wrong. I also needed to be able to express those feelings.

My hope and prayer are that this book allows others permission to dive deep into the thoughts, feelings, and questions that grief brings and people don't talk about. From denial to bargaining, to anger, to depression, to guilt of forgetting and/or moving on to acceptance, they deserve discussion. You have permission to feel and experience whatever it is you need.

You're not weak if you cry. In fact, you are strong for allowing yourself to feel and be vulnerable. You are not crazy because you just want them back. You loved and *still love* them. You are not bad or evil because you are angry with life, them, yourself, others, or God. You are human. You are not guilty and have done nothing wrong if (or when) you move forward or forget. You are finding the new you. You are not dishonoring or disrespecting because you have accepted. You are living your life.

I wrote this book for me, but I am publishing it for all of us, the grieving.

Inspiration

Inspiration through grief and death seems absurd to many, as they avoid their hurt, pain, and disbelief. I don't fault them or judge them. God knows, I did not, nor do I want to now experience the deep and hollow pain of losing my wife to cancer. It's been five years, and it still does not make sense to me. I don't think it ever will.

But, the pain of grief is real, and I was, and still am, willing to travel through it, to hopefully come out the other side and find happiness, joy, life, and me again.

Inspired by feelings, any and all of them, I write.

My true inspiration is to help with healing, mine and yours.

PREFACE: THE SEVEN STAGES OF GRIEF

1. **Shock and Denial:** A natural response to cushion the immediate impact of the loss, creating numbness or a feeling of disbelief.

2. **Pain and Guilt:** Intense feelings of sorrow, fear, anxiety, regret, and guilt may surface as the reality of the loss begins to set in.

3. **Anger and Bargaining:** Frustration and helplessness may lead to anger, while bargaining can involve thoughts of "if only" or making deals to change what happened.

4. **Depression:** Deep feelings of sadness, hopelessness, and loneliness may arise as the person begins to confront the loss.

5. **The Upward Turn:** As the intensity of grief begins to lessen, a sense of calm and new hope can emerge.

6. **Reconstruction and Working Through:** Individuals start to adapt to their new reality without the lost person or situation, learning to cope and re-engage with life.

7. **Acceptance and Hope:** This involves coming to terms with the loss and learning to live with the changed circumstances, which is not the same as "moving on," but rather finding a way forward. [1]

---

[1] This is based upon Elisabeth Kübler-Ross's original 5-Stages of Grief from her 1969 book *On Death and Dying*.

Content Warning

The following material includes references to grief, loss, depression, and suicidal ideation, which may be distressing or triggering for some readers. Please proceed with care and prioritize your well-being. If this topic is difficult for you, consider stepping away or seeking support from a trusted person or a mental health professional.

There are resources at the back of this book, should you need them.

FRACTURED MIRROR

GRIEVING BEAUTIFULLY IMPERFECT

PROLOGUE

Blue Waters

I stood at the shoreline
Gazing about the crystal blue

Swells of curiosity
Washed before me

How deep the water
How far does it extend
What life within

Filled with desire
To walk
Swim
Play
In these waters

Surrounded by

Radiant sapphire
Translucent cobalt

Captured

In waves of emotions
They crash about me

Intoxicating love
Gentle tenderness

Peace

I stood at the shoreline
Gazing about the crystal blue
Until the sands of time

Closed your eyes

Walking Beauty

She walked
no
she glided

moving effortlessly
across the floor
through the room

as if floating
just above
the hard wood floor
below

elegant and graceful
supple and agile

She was silently beautiful

Thump, scrape, slide
Thump, scrape, slide

The cane
Her foot

left foot
right foot
cane

or is it

cane
right foot
left foot
cane

Ya, that's it

the thump
the scrape
the slide
the thump

She staggered, hobbled
across the floor
through the room

each step unstable
hammering,
pounding
into
the hardwood floor
below

elegant and graceful
supple and agile

She was beautiful

DENIAL

My wife is dying
What the hell

I've been sitting in denial
For a while
It just doesn't seem real

Denial

I've been preparing for nine years
But, now it's here
And it doesn't seem real

Denial

I want to be angry
I want to rage out
But I don't have the energy

I want to cry
But how do I have enough tears

I want to get past this denial

NO

I don't want my wife to die

I want the pain to stop
Hers
Mine
The kid's

Longing for her to be at peace
I don't remember
What does peace feel like

More denial

All I feel
Pain
Dread

I know there's hope
I do believe

But right now

My wife is dying

Eight to Sixteen

My heart is warmed
joys and smiles
peace and contentment
my heart is full

Looking across the room
five amazing, beautiful children
our children
all busy doing schoolwork

From eight to sixteen
I see our gift from God
our legacy
our children

I see our future
as they sit in our present

The wonders they'll see
experience
are

In a momentary glance
time held
the beauty
of our children

In my heart

A Table Meant for Seven

I saw my future this evening
A table set for six
A table meant for seven

Each plate
Faced the other
Paired up
Across from each other
A table meant for seven

I placed each plate
Purposeful
Hesitant
Hopeful
Sorrowful
A table meant for seven

The call for dinner came
Footsteps
Chairs sliding out
Settling in
A table meant for seven

Arms extended out
Hands and hearts open
Embracing
Blessing
A table meant for seven

Chatter of the day
From eight to sixteen
I sat silent
At our table meant for seven

Grieving

Mourning
A table meant for seven

Graciously thankful
Humbled and honored

A table set for six
A table meant for seven

Love Story

I heard it said
It was a love story

Two introverts

Back row
Back table
Background

No limelight
No fuss

A simple
Love between us

Complex through the years
Yet love never failed

A simple
Love between us

Captivating
Exhilarating
Life giving

Dedicated
Promised
Ordained

We
The love story
Fractured mirror
Beautifully imperfect
Til death does part us

The time is near
Our thirty-chapter book
Now in the last chapter
Only pages to go

This quiet love story
Two introverts
Became one flesh
Tragically ending

No cliff hanger
No teaser
No sequel

Let me rest in this page
A little longer
Let my love
Carry you to the end

Let me read this story
Again
And again

May our children
Grandchildren
The world
Know
Our

Love

Labored Breathing

The whistling wheeze
The wheezing whistle

Grasping gasps
Panting puffs

Breathless breaths
Winded

Winded

Strained and labored
Exhausted

Shhhhh

The Space In-Between

Life and death

Living and dying

Living death

Death

I
MONTH
LIVE LIKE
Laurie
I

Day One

I woke this morning
Not to you

Laying in the bed next to me
Not you

Woken by the light of the day
Not by you

Sun shining through the blinds
Not you

Warmth in the air
Not in you

Eyes wide
Not you

Breath of life
Beating heart
Pulsating love
Not you

This Bedroom

I don't want to be in it

The thought of that long, long
Walk down the hallway

Dread builds up
With no horizon in sight

How did this hallway get so long

The solitary twin bed sits
Alone

New carpet
New paint
Windows
Closet
Door
Bed

How many square feet is this bedroom

Empty floor space
Empty dresser
Empty heart
Empty bed
It's cold in here

The warmth left
Between five and seven
Never to return

This bedroom

How much longer can I avoid this bedroom

How much longer

How Did This Hallway Get so Long

Walk with me
down this long, long hallway

From table meant for seven
to the bed
to shards eight to sixteen
to this bedroom

Drowning in tears of
pain
grief
death
denial
avoidance

Walk with me

I sat
at the table meant for seven
motionless and emotionless
blackened blank screen
staring at me
flat affect
detached from life

Then I got up

Weakened and wobbly knees
not so willingly
straightened
headed toward the long, long hallway

The bed
first doorway on the right
master of us
five years we loved
where we discovered the cancer
heard the diagnosis of cancer

lived with the cancer

The bed
now dismantled
like the room
like us
emptied of all our

now occupied by
bicker, bicker, bicker
shards three and four

Walk with me

Turn left
the long, long hallway
new hard wood floors
extending out and out and out
plain white walls
no pictures
no decorations
no reason why

Next doorway
shard five
now on her own
with our last family picture
on the wall next to her bed
watching over her

Walk with me

On the right
next doorway
shard two
Legos, airsoft guns, and more Legos
truly a boy's room
Walk with me

Shard one
on the left

girly with an edge
emo meets Hello Kitty

Walk with me

Only ten feet more
to go

No

I don't want to
walk any further

It's the shortest
part of the hallway
but
feels like the longest

Its new
its dark
no light yet

Just a few feet longer
down what seems
like a narrowed entrapment

Straight ahead
the door
our door

Now just my door

Stay here with me
don't make me walk
any further

I'll remain

Outside this bedroom

End of Day One

What have I done today
Other than think of you

I found myself
Aimlessly walking
Through our
(can I really say “our” anymore)
House

Even with five kids
In the house
In the same room
It seemed

Empty

Walking
More like dragging
My feet
Room to room
Making sure to avoid
This bedroom

I’m not sure how long I sat
But I sat

Staring out
Staring at my screen
Staring within
Staring nowhere

All the while
I kept waiting
Waiting

To see you in the hallway
walking out of the bathroom
sitting at the dining room table

I thought I heard you
At one point

But

No

It was an echo
Of the past

Our past

The sound of silence
Pounded and railed
Against the echo
Of your lost
Voice

What I have done today
Other than think of you

MINDFULNESS

My heart is heavy
Pushing against my chest
Breathing hurts

I'd swear there's a bug
Going around
Or I ate something bad
It feels like the pit
Of hell in my stomach

Something also seems
To be pushing
At my shoulders
Hunched and drawn in

The Jell-O in my neck
What a strange feeling
Wobbly and unstable

Head still in a fog
Disbelief and denial
Scrambled eggs and thoughts
With no salt or flavor

Eyes glazed and lazy
Yet darting, searching
Drenched with tears
Seeing nothing
But you

But
You
Are
Gone

ONE WEEK

When are you coming home?

I keep looking for you
I thought I heard you
The other day

I never noticed the echo
Throughout the house before

Intriguing how silence
Can echo

Like a vacuum
Life in the house
Seems to have been sucked out

Oh wait, that's exactly
What happened

Joy's been replaced with sadness
Smiles to tears
Laughing to weeping
Living to dying

Faded away in sleep
No more pain
No more grief
No more cancer

For you

Woken to the coldness
Of the morning

Mourning

I closed my eyes
You lay next to me

Breathing

Eyes opened
Stillness in the air
No movement
No breath

The beating of your heart
No more

Awakened
To a new life
Without you

I miss you
I love you

AHAW

Five Shards of Glass

I saw the smile upon your face
in our five shards of glass

giggle
grin
laugh

five shards of glass

Sparkling eyes of blue
greens of hazel

five shards of glass

Shattered feelings
jagged hearts
fractured edges
of five shards of glass

Beauty and joy
living and breathing
imperfectly
are five shards of glass

healing
hoping
accepting

five shards of glass

You
you live on
in

five shards of glass

Another Day Without You

I woke up early today
After five hours of sleep
I looked across the empty room
With blurry eyes
Another day without you

Rolling over
To see if you were there
By chance
By some unknown
Impossible chance
You were back
Another day without you

I showered, I think
I ate breakfast
No, wait
I did not eat
The kids ate
Yes, the kids ate
Another day without you

Some went to school
Some stayed home with your mom
I went to work
I've been out for a month now
I've missed work
Another day without you

I was welcomed
With open arms
Tears of joy
And grief
We talked
Laughed
Cried
Said goodbye
My bucket full

Another day without you

Smiles
Warmth in my heart
Joy, peace, excitement
Purpose fulfilled
Hope for tomorrow
Another day without you

I walked through the door
Ready to share my day
My bliss
The overfilling
Of my cup
With you
Another day without you

With teary eyes
I looked across the empty room

Another day without you

SLEEPLESS

Here I am

Here

Again

1:00 a.m.

Awake

Still awake

The Beauty Within

Soft spoken
Never broken

Eyes of blue
Your heart so true

Joy and peace

23 Years to 23 Days

23 years of marriage
23 days without you

23 years I loved and adored you
23 days since I heard your voice

23 years of waking next to you
Going to bed with you
Living life with you

23 days not seeing your face
Only an image
Unable to look upon you

23 years gone
23 days only beginning

Hero

Now what?

My hero's dead

She lived an amazing life
Not perfect
Imperfectly perfect

Beautifully imperfect

But now
She's gone

Yes, I know
Her memory lives on

Yes, I know
She'll always be in my heart

Yes, I know
God is in control
Sovereign

But

She was my
North
East
West
South

So

Now what?

II
MONTH
LIVE LIKE
Laurie

Forever Goodbye

Forever young
Our love
Forever young
Our marriage
Forever young
Our goodbye

No time
Long enough

From seconds to hours
From days to years

From I do
To
Death parted

No time
Long enough

Distant memory
Distant dream
Distant

Sleepless nights
Wakeless days

Time stands still
Frozen undying

In our
Forever goodbye

GONE

The bad dream
Nightmare
Night terror
That never sleeps

Never wakes

Eyes closed
Eyes open

Head shaking in disbelief

Untrue
Unreal
Incomprehensible
Deniability

Weighted chest
Pounding
Desperately
Escaping
Air

Through terrorizing breaths

Welling eyes of
Horrifying tears
Face and pillow
Drenched
Drowning

How are you gone?

Goodbye Hello

We said goodbye today
before saying hello

Surreal

Dear friend
Dear lover
Dear wife

New horizon before you
home at last
forever
with
our
Creator
Lord
God
Savior

Lead to greener
greenest
pastures

Still waters
run deep
in your goodbye

In you now

No tears
no pain
no worries

Peace
Healing
Whole

Beautifully Perfect

Forever
and
Ever

Thinking Feeling

empty house
empty bed
empty heart
empty head

alone tonight
alone tomorrow
wallow in sorrow

frustration
irritation

agitation
provocation

exasperation

This Day This Hour

In just a couple hours
our children

I

will say goodbye

to you

We've known
this day, this hour
was coming

For nine years
this day, this hour
sat in a hollow box
haunting us

We knew
one day,
one hour
we would have to open it

Avoiding, ignoring,
denying, pleading
praying
this day, this hour
would never come
wishing
the hollow box
never to be opened

Ever

Yet today
this day, this hour
the box rests in my hands

This box
This day, this hour

Sealed with ten thousand tears
about to be opened
by ten thousand more

This day, this hour
our tears will open
the flood gates
of this hollow box

You my dear
My dear wife
This box is for you
Only you

With one tear left
the box will close on
this day, this hour[2]

[2] Laurie's memorial service March 28, 2021.

TODAY

I am thankful
Trying to keep hope
Alive
In my head
My Heart
As I live out today

Walking in the
Here and now

Today is a new day

I live and breathe
The air God provides
Today

Around me
About me
Within me

His sustaining breath
Lives out
The hope in me

Yesterday
Tomorrow

Distant
Beyond my grasp

Breath of life
Sustaining breath of life
Breathe in me
Today

Without You

We said goodbye today
seems so surreal

How could we say
goodbye
so early
so soon

Together
30-some years
yet not enough

How could I say goodbye to you
ever

Sure, there's life, hope
on the other side
in time this will be behind us
A distant memory

But now
right now

How can that be

I said goodbye to a dear old friend today

My best friend
My love
My wife
My life
My

Looking forward
moving forward
without you

How do those two words

go together
without you

no

NO

NO

TODAY'S A NEW DAY

Another new day
A day without you
Yet
It's still a new day
With possible
Hopes
Dreams
Adventures
Even grief

This new day
While unknown
Unwanted
Is still
A new day

How many faces will I see today
How many
Smiles
Tears

How many lives will be moved
Challenged
Stagnant

How many feelings
Will I feel
How many thoughts
Will I think

Tears of grief
Swirl between tears of joy
Droplets of
Truth and hope
Pool together
To rain
And reign

Surrounded by
Family, friends
Coworkers, clients
What will this new day bring
What will I bring

Lying before me
Beside me
Even behind me
The potential
Of this new day

Searching

Myself seems lost
Where is my self
Really, where is it
When did I lose it

Maybe it was never lost

Giving you a portion of me
Became giving my whole self
Willing I gave

Was it too much for me
You, the keeper of me
Me, the keeper of

Now I see
I see the empty hole
Within the whole

I feel the hollow space
That "should" be
Hallow

Unfulfilled
On a deserted
Isolated
Island
In the middle
Of nowhere
And everywhere
Sitting by
Myself
Beside
My
Self
Searching

A Love Story

How many love stories have I heard
Movies, shows, books
Family, friends
Can they be numbered
Numbered like sand
Counted
Counted like the stars
How many

A love story ordained
By the Creator
Before time

Destined and predestined

From my eyes' first sight
To your lung's last breath

Two flesh
We lived
We loved
Became one

We were
One

Where the story begins
Ends

Numbered were our days
Your days

Like sand and stars
We lived
We loved
We were

Silenced

Looking forward
Sitting in silence
Seeing a future
Lived out
Now

Living
Surviving
Existing

Standing upright

Longing to thrive
Again
To have the heart
My heart filled
Abundant
Overflowing

But silence

Where are you
Where did your voice go

What once was
Prevalent
Inspiring
Stretching from the past
To the future
While grounded in
The here and now

Is

Silent among the darkness

Darkened by the light of day
Exposing truth
Your truth
Reality that cannot be

Denied
Escaped

Silent truth
From sun to Son
Unending
Unbending
Time

Contemplating

1:44 a.m.
Yes, 1:44 in the morning

What the hell am I doing up

Contemplating

Life
Death

Living
Surviving
Thriving

Where am I

Drifting floating
Falling drowning

Not sleeping

Certainly not dreaming

Apparently the dream died

Figuratively
Literally

Gone

Forever separated
Forever 1:44 a.m.

The clock ticks
The hands move
Ever so slowly
Tick, tick, tick
Not a single tock

Frozen in time
As it warps by
In an endless
Groundhog Day
Loop

Forget about
Her
Move on
With your life

Really

Every dream
Movie
Love story
Poem

Her

About her
For her
To her
Her

Contemplating
Life without

Her

At 1:44 a.m.
Yes
At 1:44 in the morning

Parties

Another party without you
How many more parties do we—

No wait

There is no more we
Is there

Only I

I

How many more parties do

I

Have to endure
Without
You

Birthdays
Anniversaries
Holidays

Any day

All days

How many more?

ISOLATED

In the smallness
of
this colossal world

Kids, parents
aunts, uncles,
grandparents
friends
coworkers

Too many to count
abundantly overflowing
blessings each day

Curing the isolation
the isolated one

One
Only one

Isolated in isolation

In the corner
curled up with this laptop
my only solace

The words before me
staring at me
through my soul
to the emptiness
I feel

To the emptiness I have become

Words before me
words dragging behind
words yet to come

Isolated words
keeping me company

Speaking to me
whispering howls
screaming tears
surround me in this isolated

Bubble

This corner of my world
amongst the living
while death
wreaks havoc inside
my head and heart

Gripping death
ha, death...[3]

Refusing to let go
memories tied
to the death of life

I sit here
in this

---

[3] A nod to the poem "Dripping" from Book I.

Faces Faces Faces

All these faces
in all these places
miles and miles
of smiles
eyes ears mouths nose
nobody knows

The blind
The deaf
The mute
The anosmic

longing for connection
for resolution
absolution
all these faces
in all these places

None
are
you [4]

---

[4] Inspired by the book "Hand, Hand, Fingers, Thumb.

III
MONTH
LIVE LIKE
Laurie

Finding My Happy

Dwelling on where it went
Why it went
Asking a billion questions
Being halfway there
What purpose does it serve

In the end
I'm still here
Without my happy

The grief
The sadness
The depression

All thrive
Without my happy

Exclaiming in tears of joy
When I grovel in tears of pain

Feeding their empty soul
Draining my breath of life

How easily it happens
Setting out to write about my happy
Several lines later
Still writing about
Without

Obsessive dwelling
Preoccupied preoccupation
Intrusive thoughts

Randomly habitualized
To normalized

The unwanted

Without

Is that what my happy has been reduced to

Without

How sad

And now
I am
sad

I Sat

I pulled into the parking lot, like it was any other day. Just another day at work. Another day where I get to do what I love. A day of being blessed by being a blessing. Another day to do what God has called me to do. A day to follow Him. His leading. His still small voice. His lion's roar. Another day at doing what I love and where I love it.

I found my normal spot, closest one to the gate. Parked my car. Turned off the engine. Opened the driver's door. Left leg went out. Foot planted on the asphalt. Hands fell into my lap. Frozen in my seat.

I sat.

Weighed down by some unseen force, I sat unmoving. I felt the weight. I felt nothing. Motionless and lifeless. Staring out into dead air. Dead space. Eyes glazed over by the blackness before me. Behind me. Beside me. Beyond me. Strapped to the seat by a belt that felt more like iron clad chains. Bound. Tied. Gagged. Imprisoned.

I sat.

Emptied heart and head broken by death. Sucked the life out of me. Out of her.

I sat.

Into a vacuum went the colors of my heart, my life. Layers upon layers of exuberant colors flowed before me, behind me, beside me, beyond me. Now gone. Staring out into the gray dull, feeling its weight. Feeling it's lack. It's emptiness.

I sat.

Noticing nothing. Blinded and bound. Hearing only echoes of the past in the silence of my head. Motivated. Inspired. Moved. Stirred. Stimulated. Encouraged. Driven. By nothing.

I sat.

No tears. No yells. No screams.
Numb
I sat

Time was lost
Nonexistent
The beat of my heart broke the moment
A slow drawn breath broke the silence
For another beat
I sat

Then I got up

Writings

Last thing I ever wanted in my life
was to walk this road

No matter what the road looked or felt like
No matter what road we were on
No matter what the road was
Alone

And yet
life and death have a way of mirroring each other at times
they seem to be opposites and companions at the same time

Living in the pain of grief
can be strangely beautiful

There's a painful elegance that comes
only
through the process

Grieving what's been lost
hopeful for the future
even the here and now

Hopeless Romantic
lost in dreams
dreamer dreaming wonders of awe
the beautifully imperfect

Silence

At times
deafening and torturous
At times
peaceful and tranquil

There's a cold, frightening silence
when the pursuer
pursues the avoider

The silence of a spouse
desperately longing
to hear from the other
only to be met with
silent indifference

There's a calm, peaceful silence
as the ocean swells roll in
just before crashing against the rocks

the silence of my wife being gone is maddening

I have music
I have poetry
I have five shards

Family
Friends
Work

All good things

But at the end of the night
I have silence

Walking the Road

This road
Mirrored by
The beauty of life
The fracture of death
Opposing, defying opposites
Completing, fulfilling companions
The strange awkward
Beauty in grief

A
Painful
Hopeful
Process

Dreams and nightmares
Of yesterday
Yesteryear

Dreams and nightmares
The future
The here
The now
The possibilities

The unknown

Long is the road
Twisted

Widened by the narrows
Straighten by the curves
Shortened by the beauty
Lengthened by the fractured

Pick your lane
Right, left
Fast, slow
Turning, driving

Any number you want

You still won't want it

The lane
The road
The fracture
The death

Unavoidable
Unimaginable
Unpreventable
Inescapable
Inevitable

Road
of
Grief

Happy Birthday

Today's another day
Another day
Another day

A day of celebration
Celebrating
Life and Life

One day
Many days ago
This was a day to celebrate
We celebrated
We

One day
Many more days ago
It was nineteen
Golden day
Depressing
Depressing [5]

One day
Today
What is today
Another day
Another day

Without you
Another day
Another day

Without you
Another day
Without you

[5] This refers to my poem "Nineteen on the Nineth" from Book I.

Happy Birthday II

Today came and went
Another day
Another day

A day of celebration
I celebrated
My life
My life

One day
On this one day
New beginning
Hope
Hope

One day
Many days from now
I'll celebrate
Again
Again

Today
This day
Without you
You
You

Random Moment

Saw a picture of you today
randomly
from social media

You were smiling
your authentic smile
eyes illuminating

I could see the joy
within you
coming out of you

naturally

A whirlwind
spiraling before me

Your smile
your eyes
your joy

I had to close the picture
I could not look
any
longer

MONTH
LIVE LIKE
Laurie

The Bed

I saw the bed
where we used to sleep
cuddled behind you
right arm draped over you
hand grabbing your shoulder
pulling you in tight

My face resting
just behind yours
my nose buried in your hair
now settling for the smoothness
of your bald head

I saw the bed
where hours we spent
talking
listening
stories being told
hearts and lives
being shared

I saw the bed
where you comforted me from
depression
anxiety
the darkness with me

I saw the bed
where we woke
each morning
together
you, right where you fell asleep
me, anywhere on the bed

I saw the bed
where I loved you
day in and day out

I saw the bed
where we discovered the cancer
heard the diagnosis of cancer
lived with the cancer
died from the cancer

I saw the bed
where we loved
loved each other
each day
each night
each

AHAW

Another Family Party

I stopped for a moment
today
only for a moment
that's all I had
A moment
today

I saw you scurrying
around the house
arranging
forks, knives, spoons
setting
plates, bowls, napkins
stacking
cups

I saw you
walking, hobbling
step, slide, thump
from room to room
making sure it was
just right

Another birthday
another family party
another
and another

And just like that
in the blink and wink
of an eye
the moment was gone
and so were you

Thirty years with you
104 days without you

Thirty years in a flash

104 days inching by
slower than a snail's pace

Still questioning
how this happened
how could this possibly happen
to us
to you
to me

Til death do us part
realer than real

All in this moment
that's all I had
A moment
today

With
Out
You

Muse

Sitting
Staring
At an empty
Screen

Feelings
Mixed
Knotted
Voided

Happy sad mad
Numb

Random words
Thrown together
Negated assortment

Empty page
Empty head
Empty heart
Empty soul

Drained by the flood
Flooded by the drain

No more
No more muse

Words
Music
Inspiration
Feelings

Lost in the ashes
Of my muse

Sitting
Staring
At an empty
Screen

My Muse

My inspiration
Lifting my spirits
Exceeding my dreams
Brilliant shooting star
Fiery blaze
Streaking through
The darken night
Dazzling, dispersion
Spreading sparkles
Across the heavens
My muse
Music to my soul
Notes dancing
Upon the score
Keys and strings
Chords and melody
Caesura [6]

You were

[6] *Caesura* - the timely pause in my heartbeat. The strategic silence that took my breath away in the presence of my muse.

It's Good to Have Everyone Here

Everyone
Everybody

Everyone but you
No longer here
No longer everybody

Everyone
Everybody

I hate these words

Pain, sorrow, grief, loneliness
Alone, without, empty, gone

Anything but
Everyone
Everybody

The impossible
But unescapable

Truth

Not
Everyone

Not
Everybody

Is here

Grief vs. Depression

What is it
Grief
Depression

Lethargic
Blah

Foggy brain
Foggy thoughts
Foggy feeling

Numbed sadness
Sadden numbness

Tears in my eyes
Lacking the energy to fall

Movement driven
But asleep at the wheel

Fear of this
Fear of that

Hope for neither

Sitting
Staring

Blood
Coursing flowing

Somewhere
Nowhere

Not anywhere
Not everywhere

Tears welling
Still not falling

Building pooling
Surrounding blinding

Still not falling

Quick breath in
Forced breath out

Building

Slow breath in
Controlled breath out

Pushed away
Under the rug
Into the trash can

Down deep
Avoidance

Head hung
Low

All in the name of
Loneliness

Sleepless Nights

Sleepless nights
When does my loneliness end
The days of isolation
The nights of seclusion

Sleepless nights
Nights *resounding* with nothing
But silence

Sleepless nights
Filled with the chatter of
Music, tv, podcast
Anything to remove
The silence

Sleepless nights
Echoing the multitude
Of words in my head

Sleepless nights
Tears flowing
Yells and screams
Muffled in my pillow

Sleepless nights
Hope distant, lost

Sleepless nights
With no perceived end

Sleepless nights

How the Hell is this Okay?

You promised me
Yes, I know it was nearly ten years ago
But you promised me

Your words,
"Everything is going to be okay
in the end."

Well, I'm not okay

She's dead
How the hell is this okay

Do you hear me
(anger welling)

Where are you?
(anger boiling)

I'm not fucking okay
(full guttural yell)

(dead air)

I'm not okay
(whispered through tears)

Where are you
(barley audible)

Crickets

Where are you
How the hell is this okay
(anger rising)

For years I longed
For years I searched

For years I envisioned
The dream
My dream

Love
Twenty-some years gone by
And the dream became reality
With this ring, I thee wed
You gave me my dream
Laid before my eyes

To walk hand and hand
Together
To grow old
Together

All to have you take her away from me?

Really?

How is this right
How is this real

How the hell is this okay

Its not fair
No, really
Its not fair

I heard the blasphemous rumors
Are they just rumors
They have to be

What the hell am I supposed to do now?

Your words,
"Everything is going to be okay
In the end."

Falling
folding

Collapsing

Deadweight to nothing

(muted tears)
But I'm not okay

My Phone

How many times did I check my phone today
willing it to come to life
light up
buzz
any resemblance of hope

Consumed by

One thought
One name
One face

Each bright light
Each movement
Each sound

Only dimmed
in silent
disappointment

The endless wondering
if it were you
could it be you
would it be

You

The endless wandering
of my thoughts
feelings
of you

And yet
That damn yet

Yet was not coming

Silence

Silenced by
miles of eternity
A future
that is not

Yes, how many times did I check my phone today

Wishing to see your name
hear your voice
feel your love

Six to Two

How is it possible
Reality
Fantasy

Either or
Both and

Feelings felt
Connected connection
Silence silenced

Acceptance
Authentic acceptance
No walls
No hiding
No avoiding
No reservation

Pouring in
Pour out

Pouring
Within
About
Around
Throughout

The totality
No duality
Complete
Congruency

Solely
Merely
Purely

Simply you
Simply me

Broken

The road before me
The road behind me

Twists
Turns
Twenty-some
Thirty

Like branches from the trunk
Five roads go about their own
Directions unknown
Changed for all
Changed forever

Split by lighting
The trunk to never grow again
From road work ahead
To no U-Turn Ahead

Dead-end

Potholes
Fainted painted lines
Knots in the tree
Branches pruned

Bulldozers and chainsaws
Destroy what once was [7]

The lonely road
The lonely stump

---

7 "What Once Was" is a poem from my first book, describing my dream of love and the loss of it; foreshadowing what was to come forty some years later.

Never to grow
Never to live
Never to change

Remaining

For all to see
For all to forget

For all to...

V
MONTH
LIVE LIKE
Laurie

15 South

Hazy dazy lazy clouds
Swimming in and about
Intertwined

Thick in the midst
Of more than mist
Wading through

Step-by-step
Inch by inch
Leap by leap

This cloudy day
This overcast cloudy day

And yet

A sliver
A crack
A fracture

Shadow of light
Peeking creeping
Shining blinding

Hope arises

Looking Forward

Why is my heart beating
Just a bit faster than normal

I feel the ever-so-slightly
Rapid thumping in my chest

Like a butterfly escaping its cage
For the first time

Flying this way
That way
Sideways
There's an energy
Raising in my chest
I cannot explain

How many butterflies are in there

Weighted
Is my chest
Weighted with anticipated wonder

What is
What could be

The thump thumping
Increasing speed
Intensity

Lightened freedom
Awaited hope

Rushes by
In slow motion

On each beat
Each breath

Wings of the butterfly
Foreshadowing
The racing

Heart
Thoughts
Desires

HOLD ON—LET GO

I remember you
Your face
Your smile
Your eyes

Oh, your eyes
Those deep blue waters [8]
Intriguing
Captivating
Drawing me in
Closer
Closer still

Your sweet tender lips
Speaking life's truths
Love and compassion
Soft to touch
To kiss

Fading
Is my memory

No longer can I
Hear your voice
Minutes turn to days

I fear days are turning to weeks

What began as forever
Has now become never

Each tear shed
Seems to wash away
The pain
The grief

---

[8] A nod back to the first poem of the book, "Blue Waters." These feelings are not linear. Grief is not linear.

The loss

The memory
Of you

Guilt for memories lost
Guilt for letting go
Guilt for moving forward

Even guilt for losing you

Let go
Let go

Good Morning

Woke to the beauty of
Today and all it brings

Morning rays
Beaming smiles
Joyful peace

Woke to the anticipation
Hope for tomorrow

Dancing butterflies
Blushing giggles
Adventures new

What will today
This day
Bring

What will I bring

Wishing
Dreaming

Dreaming

Tomorrow
Ever so close
Yet still beyond

And you
Yes you

Where will you be

Wishing
Dreaming

Let flowers

Blossom bloom
Let butterflies
Freely fly

Together connected
You and I

TORN

Torn between two
One flesh and blood
The other not

One
Sunflower smile
Sparkling eyes
Hair afire
Full of life
The other
A dream
So long ago
Yet just yesterday
Passed

Torn

Feelings of grief
Feelings of exhilaration
Tears of sadness
Yesterday and today
Even now
Here and now
Butterflies of anticipation
Yesterday and today
Even now
Here and now

Torn

Future and past
Collide
Unknown
Undecided
Unresolved

Torn

First Kiss

He stood before her
Their feet inches apart
His: shuffling nervously to and fro
Hers: light and airy
Bouncing with the fullness of life

A timid step forward, by him
Closing the gap between
Opening the space to be

Outstretched wide, her arms
Wrapping drawing
Him in

Uncertain, cautious disbelief
His hands round her waist
Welcoming her arms draped over him

Embraced

Time
Moment
Each other

Quick like a cat
Her lips upon his neck

And then gone

Stunned dazed
In the thrilling cloud
Forming within

Arms now loose
By their sides
Feet stepping back

But then

Momentary courage
Push
Daring his feet forward

His arms reaching out
Longing to hold her
Embrace again

Tight

Again, her soft lips meet
His neck

Pulling back
The space to be
He stares

Entranced
Enthralled
Ensnared

Captivated
Fascinated

Her lips

Glistening
Gleaming
Glimmering

Luminous

Looking up
Eyes meet

His hand
Cradling hers

Flirting
Fingers

Warm
Willing

Gently
Playfully

Tracing
Each one

Her hand
At home
Resting in his

Again, her lips

Tempting the space between
His lips meet hers

Gently pressing
Resting within

Eyes meeting again
No words spoken

Their lips

Passionately

Intertwined
Interwoven

Enmeshed
Entangled

His hand rising
Caresses her cheek

With one more
Kiss [9]

---

[9] My first kiss after Laurie's passing. A formidable moment.

Drawn to You

Brilliantly beautiful
Baffling
Vibrant and vivacious

Face of freckles
Eyes exotic
Moistened
Lustrous lips

Authentically
Genuinely
Vulnerable

Investing
Nesting
Resting

Peace

Good
Bad
Other

Breath of
Fresh air

Chose
Choice
Chosen

Yes

Emotional
Reasonable
Rational
Skittish

Strong enough

To be
Weak

Feeling deep
Deeply feeling

Profound Passion
Heart
Mind
Soul

About
Around
Accompanying

Flesh and blood
Real

Fantastically
Real

Drawn to you
Drawn to me
Drawn to us

Someday

She said I was handsome
She said I was a sweetheart
She said she had feelings
For me

But, she could take it back

She laughed at my jokes
She listened to my heart
She heard my space in-between

But, she could take it back

She was vulnerable
She was authentic
She was congruent

But, she could take it back

She smiled with me
She flirted with me
She cried with me

But, she could take it back

She embraced me tightly
She held my hand gently
She kissed me tenderly

But, she could take it back

She gazed
She hoped
She trusted

Will she

When Did You Know

First date
At a glance
Locking of eyes

The hello hug
Casual and quaint
Accidental legs brushing
Under the table
Lingering for just a moment longer

Your laugh as you
Playfully hit my forearm
Throughout dinner

Our first, second, or third
Hug goodbye
Not wanting to let go

Nestling your hand in mine
Fingers interweaved
Melting into one another
Intimacy

The innocent tenderness
Of our first kiss

The passionate heat
Of our second

Giggling mind spinning
Blood rushing
Walking on air
Butterflies flying
Astounded amazement
Normalcy normalized
Deniability denied

It just felt right

VI
MONTH
LIVE LIKE
Laurie

Our Marriage

The slow deep breath in
The long-drawn breath out

Freely given
Freely taken

Hands extended
Hands clasped

Two hands

Touch
Pressed together
Can't let go of each other
Won't let go
It means too much [10]

Fingers
Hearts
Lives

Intertwined
Interwoven

Two flesh become one
Life lived

Then
Labored breathing

Breathless
Winded
Strained

The setting sun

---

[10] A nod to the first poem Laurie ever wrote about us, "Two Hands" in Book I.

The setting life

The death does part us
The last breath

The rising morning
The rising soul

The end
Freely given
Freely taken

7-26-21

Today would have been our 24th wedding anniversary.

It's been a little more than five months since you passed away. It still seems so unreal. Some days I don't notice, with the new normalcy - settling in. Other days I can hardly breathe, stuck in the brainless fog of denial.

Me being me...I find myself stuck between the questioning of why and the knowing of why, the guilt of being in the past and the guilt of moving forward, the life I don't want (never wanted) and the excitement of the life to come.

Go figure. I live in the dualities of my heart and mind.

I was asked yesterday, "What do I miss?" There are so many things, but I think most of all, I miss my best friend. I miss being known and loved by you on that level. No other relationship can compare to that of husband and wife.

The road to find my "new" happy and my new "me" has been bittersweet (again, more dualities, LOL). I know I'm not alone and many have traveled this road before me and many will travel it after me. But this is my road and the unknown of my road can be unbearable, just as it is hopeful.

Are we seeing a pattern here?

I am determined to see and experience the wholeness of my grief, as difficult as it may be. My cup is neither half full nor half empty. It truly is both!! I grieve and hope in the same heartbeat, breath, blink of an eye. Even now. Even today. I grieve. I hope. This very moment.

What an oddity. And yet, Christ Jesus has not only given me permission, but He Himself set the example of being *real* and allowing a time for everything.

My intent, my goal, even my dream, is to sit in the suck, the muck, the mire, and then rise on the wings of the dawn as my steps carry me through the leading of His Spirit to my new life that was/is ordained by Him (just as my old life was ordained by Him).

Now on this day, this wonderfully horrible day (or is it horribly wonderful day) I will grieve. I will cry (already did). I will rejoice. I will thank God. I will praise God. I will hope. I will love. I will live. I will live for today. I will live with yesterday. I will live for tomorrow. I will live.

Yes.

I will live.

24 Years

I remember
I don't want to remember

The numb fog
Unseen
Yet blinding

The pain
The weighted pain
Burdened by the yoke
Of your death

Oh death, where is your sting

Pinching, piercing, penetrating
My heart
My thoughts
My life

Six feet
Ashes to ashes
Dust to dust
Until death part us

And it did

Just as assured
Just as promised
Just as ordained

Where has death left me
Wondering and wandering

Feelings overwhelmed
Chaotic

Thoughts scattered
Lost

Actions undone
Void

Apathetically drowning
Hopeless

Still searching
Waiting for you
To come home

To see your face
Hear your voice
Feel your touch

Only to reside
In the undeniable
Denial
Of this now
My life

Right or wrong
Good or bad
Healthy or not
Rational or not

Death's sting
Your death
Stings

Death's Sting

A hole opened up within the center of my chest
just below my ribcage
the hole of emptiness
the whole of grief

It's like this nervous ball of energy
spinning a million miles an hour
barbed wire and razor blades
surround the circumference
protecting the hollow emptiness within

The words
death, pain, sorrow, silence
ever falling and flowing about the hole

It hurts
somatic pain
real
not imagined

It shortens and quickens my breath
at the same time

I can feel the air
forced out
eliminated, expelled, ejected
banished
by the hole
escaping out of my mouth

I can feel the oxygen
forced in
franticly, feverishly, fearfully
anxiously
racing in slow motion though my windpipe
longing to fill the hole

I feel the walls around the oxygen
as they swell with increasing pain
foreshadowing an even deeper pain to come
the hole shifts ever-so-slightly
but feels like a ten-thousand-foot freefall
to my stomach

Like a slingshot or trampoline
it bounces to my upper chest
just below my neck

Tears begin to form from the pain
and fear

Blood races to my head
my breathing matching it
flushed face
watering eyes
pounding ears
locked jaw
weakened arms

How am I still typing
As I feel this now
Yes, even now
Right now

It hurts
I don't want to feel this anymore
Please make it stop
Please stop
Please stop
Stop
End

End the pian
End the madness

End

Sinking

At what point does mercy's grace
surpass the drowning wave before me
the slow drowning

When does the breath of heaven
fill my waterlogged
smoke filled lungs

Dying to self
Dying to the world
Dying to them

Dying to You

hopeless thoughts
hopeless feelings
Drive this
hopeless behavior
drowning this
hopeless life

Mercy and Grace
Wisdom and discernment

Where are you

I need you
I need You now

Dry bones
creaking
crackling

Fracturing
beneath the weight

Guilt and shame

Drenched
Drowned
Slowly

Old and New Memories

Packing snacks for a 1000-mile trip
the overnight bag that's too full
but still missing something

Driving the Colorado mountain road
our song or songs
randomly played on the radio
listening to U2

The silly car conversations
the made-up games

The overnight dive motel
with five tired children

Taking the motel
soap, shampoo, Kleenex, toilet paper

and now...

Going to bed alone
waking alone

All the little things I notice
that I cannot share with you

My daydreams pondering
deep thoughts that now remain
lost between my heart and head
and five tired shards

New Hands

Time frozen
Anew

Cuddling gently
Calmly resting within

Interlacing playfully
Flirtatiously teasing

Gripping firmly
Securely refusing to let go

Time frozen
Anew

Fingers to cheek
Edging down

Palm upon chin
Resolved

Caressing forehead
Ceaselessly committed

Burrowing
Fingers through hair

Time frozen
Anew

Nuzzled skin to skin
Small of the back

Interlocking enmeshment
Back of the neck

Fingers palms
Forever kissed

Time frozen
Anew

New feelings
New meanings
New hands

Time frozen
Anew

Mourning

Let's get married
really

Hopeless romantic
Bleeding heart
Dead poet

Marry me
really

Dreamer
Silly little dreamer
Starry-eyed
Blind man

With this ring I thee wed
really

Complete me
Two flesh become one

Til death does part us
really

Idealist
Optimist
Sentimental fool

Not today
really

MONTH
LIVE LIKE
Laurie

Releasing You into That Good Night

Softly whispered
Cupping your hand
Stroking your forehead
Gently given

Words spoken
Stories told
Memories shared
Confessions voiced
Forgiveness asked
Grace given

Here and now
Time is short
Slipping away

Letting you go
Tears cried
Promises made

Desperate plea
Don't leave me

Weeping
Wailing

Come back
Come back to me

Cries to Heaven
Head buried
Begging
Bargaining
Pleading

Come back
Come back to me

Tear drenched eyes
Swollen
Redden
Broken

Turning of the last page
Bubbling gurgling breath

Straining
Slowing
Ending

One last kiss
One last goodbye
One last I love you
One last AHAW

Goodnight
Goodbye

The Ledge

50 feet
60 feet
Maybe 100 feet
Didn't really matter
It was enough
Enough to do the job

Floating feet
Gliding toward

The Ledge
The Edge
The End

As is if nothing mattered
A means to an end

The end

Not a slight subtle glance
But a sudden savory gaze
Longing to be known
To know
The end

Forever starts now

How long did I stare
Down the unknown

50 feet
60 feet
100 feet

Wishing
Willing
Begging

The end
To meet the means

End [11]

[11] NEEDTOBREATHE concert Sept 14, 2021. Standing at the ledge. A painful, but pivotal night for me.

Walking Across the Wounded Wreckage

Writing seems so foreign to me now
I sit. I stare. I blink. I blank.
Cocking my head in searching wonder
As I wander through the space between

Emptied. Hollowed-out. Gutted.
White screen—now black
Black letters—now white
The same, but different

The shaking of my head
The stillness of the keys
The echoing silence of words that disappear before audible
No ears to hear. No eyes to see. No mouth to speak.

Cracked. Broken. Shattered. [12]

Not knowing what is next
The unknown. The unpredictable. Mysterious void.
Unidentified solitude solidifying unfamiliarity

The UNs.

Mercy's shore
Somewhere, somehow in the distance
I don't know

The buzzing of my head
The buzzing fly
The buzzing of my light
The buzzing silence

Walking to crawling
Letters to words to letters

[12] Chapters 3, 4, & 5 in Book I.

Faking It

For an hour
I faked being happy

60 minutes
Talking
Smiling
Interacting

Pretending to be

Not what I am
Not what I feel

Life flipping the light switch

It went on

Mouth smiling and grinning
Eyes open and bright
Voice chipper and cheerful

Engaging
Interacting
Inviting

It went off

Mouth droopy and drawn
Eyes cold and lifeless
Voice strained and blah

Shutoff
Shutdown
Shut up

Done—Be Done

Can't wait for this day to be over

This week
This month
This year

Screw it

This life

Waking Up

It's another Sunday morning
And you're not here
I woke up dreading the day
Longing for the weekend to be over
To end the stretched-out ticking of time
That never stops

My eyes swarm
Full of memories
Of you
As they refuse to open

The light
The day
Call it fate
Prying them open
To see the emptiness
Of a full life
Without you

MONTH
LIVE LIKE
Laurie

Empty

Heavy was the weight of emptiness
Pushing upon my shoulders

Shoving
Crushing
Heaving

Overwhelming
Overpowering

Relentless

Burdened
Mass

Yoked
Control

Relentless

Heavy was the emptiness of the weight
Shouldering upon my push

When

arrow
gun
baseball bat

Any should do the trick

bridge
cliff
giant staircase

Any should do the job

knife
car
bottle of pills

Any should serve the purpose

when does it end

by natural causes
by self-infliction

Death comes

just not soon enough

sometimes

Upsiding Down I

How quickly
Things change

And yet
Remain the same

Standing in hysteria
Running in peace

Shards say
The same but different

Love and loss
Lost in love

Dueling
Dualities

Fragile
Strength

Rightening up
Upsiding down

Beautifully
Fractured

Happy
Tears

She's all

Upsiding Down II

She's all

Tears
Happy

Fractured
Beautifully

Upsiding down
Rightening up

Strength
Fragile

Dualities
Dueling

Lost in love
Love and loss

The same but different
Shards say

Running in peace
Standing in hysteria

Remain the same
And yet

Things change
How quickly

Mystery

I followed you into our mystery
30 years being loved by you
Following anywhere, everywhere

But not here

With one last gurgling breath
You slipped into the mystery

No longer joined
No longer two flesh become one
No longer following

No longer our mystery

Where do I go from here
Where do I follow
Where do I lead
Where is my mystery

Blindly I stand
Blindly I stumble
Blindly I crawl

A vertical fall
Into this mystery

Unknowing
Unwilling
Unending

Into my mystery

TSUNAMI

Wave after wave
Grief
Loneliness
Isolation

Each wave seemly
Higher
Wider
Deeper

Towering beyond what
I thought was possible

Knit closely together
The space in-between
Almost nil

No time to breathe
Lungs imploding
Tears exploding
No desire to breathe

Drowning in the bitter
Salted waves of tears

GRIEF

Grief is real
Grief is painful
Grief is long lasting

Grief is unpredictable
Grief is being human

Grief is strength
Grief is not weakness

Grief is shared by all
Grief is known by all

Grief is love
Grief is inevitable
Grief is REAL

IX
MONTH
LIVE LIKE
Laurie

Music Died

How is it that a simple
song
chord
note
Will twist my stomach so

Breath quickly escapes
leaving an emptiness

I know all too well

The hollowed lungs
of a hollowed-out heart
foreshadowing
the hollowing
of life itself

Emptied and forgotten
abandoned and withered

Like the dying rose

Petals drooping
falling, fallen
drained of all life

Wasted

The notes turn to chords
the chords turn to song
the song turns to ash

Deep is the breath of life
heavy is the sigh of death

Weighted is the heart
wet is the tear
grief is the morn

Is the

Song
Chord
Note

Death Stood

Death stood
Feet firmly planted
Silently swaying
To and fro

Hissing

Sinister, vile words
Whispered over his talons
Slithering off freshly sharpened clawed wings

Death stood
Flickering forked tongue
Tantalizingly tickling
The bended ear

Beckoning closer
Closer still
Drawing in
Drawing near

Summoning
Bidding at his behest

Roaring

Resounding resentment
Reprimanded berated chastised

Hellish hounds
Snarl through gritted teeth
Dripping drooling
Spittle

Death stood
behind me
beside me
With me

Marbleized

Marbled cracks changing through time

Past
Present
Future

Empty void of resounding silence

Creeping
Crawling
Inching
Leaping
Solidified
Petrified
Marbleized

LAURIE

I still cry out your name

In awe and wonder
In utter disbelief

In the soulful tears
That seem to have no soul

Shaking my head
As if it'll all disappear
Or I'll wake from the
Terrorizing numbness
Of this silent nightmare

Only to open my eyes
Time gone by

Feeling the

Vicious
Voided
Vacant

Hole that separates

Dream
Reality
Nightmare

The endless name
The endless love

The endless
AHAW

Looking Back Today

It rained today
I cried today
No more Resounding Praise [13]

Love's first kiss
Denied by three

Twenty-some years
Blessed Oceans [14]

Five little shards
Not so little now

Cutting their own path

Cancer
Kissing our last kiss

The last day of
Resounding Praise

---

[13] The day before Laurie passed away, her handbell choir (Resounding Praise) played a mini concert in our back yard for Laurie. It was the last time Resounding Praise has played together.

[14] A nod to Laurie's memorial service. Shards 3 & 5 and two cousins sang "Oceans" by Hillsong

X
MONTH
LIVE LIKE
Laurie

Missing Mark

Where did he go
How long will he be gone
When will he get back

Will he ever return
If he does return,
Will he be the same

I guess not
How could he be the same
What will be different

Passions
Desires
Loves
Likes

Dislikes
Annoyances
Frustrations
Hates

His music
His writing
His vision

His heart
His mind
His him

I see

Bits and pieces
Glimpses
Here and there

I do miss him, though

Process

Standing just to fall
Falling not knowing

How far
How long
How to get up

Fall
Falling
Fallen
Fell

Laying there

Seconds
Minutes
Hours
Days
Weeks
Months
Years

Now what
Get up
When
Now

Right now

Lifting head
Pushing hands underneath
Bending knees
Supporting legs
Firming up feet
Arching back
Straightening self

Standing

Daring You to Move

Brain fog
Hazy dazy lazy
I was fuzzy then
I am fuzzy now

Cloud cover above
Gray dark rainy

Streaming down
Drizzle to pouring
Bringing more
Slush

Giving Thanks

For the life
For the death
For the space between

So much
So little
So long
So done

The dreams dreamt
The dreams lived
The dreams undone

From beginning to end
Start to finish
Dust to dust

Thanks be given
Thanks be given

WRITE ABOUT

Why don't you write about happy stuff

Birdies, bunnies, babies
Duckies, doggies, daffodils
Showering shining suns
Likes, loves, lives

No
Instead, you write about

Graphic grief
Despairing depression
Resenting rage
Anguishing anxiety
Angst anger
Helpless hopelessness
Despondent death

Yes
This is what I write about

I

Write

What

I

Feel

What Do You Want Me to Give You, Lord?

My heart
it's Yours
My mind
it's Yours

My day
it's Yours
My life
it's Yours

My kids
they're Yours

My job
it's Yours
My money
it's Yours

My wife
she's Yours

What's left

My faith

My patience
My waiting
My unknown

My pain
My grief
My loneliness

My cracked
My broken
My fractured

My unconditional belief

My being still
My knowing

Shall I play for You
Shall I play my best for You

My honor
My glory
For You

The beating drum of my
Heart
Tears
Feet
Voice

All

MONTH
LIVE LIKE
Laurie

Where Are You

In the midst
In a cloud
In the thin air

Where are you

In the darkness
In the shadows
In the daylight

Where are you

In the silence
In the multitude of voices
In the whisper

Where are you

In the crowded
In the isolation
In the somebody

Where are you

My heart
My head
My body

Emptied
Depleted
Spent

Hurting
Aching
Numb

Where are you

Crying out in
Tears
Wails
Silence

Where are you

Christmas Mourn

Christmas morn
2 a.m.
The stockings are stuffed
Five of seven
Two missing

Yours
Mine

Outside
In the trunk
They sit
Empty

No

The Road

Fearless I walked into the unknown
Without fear
I walked, ran, and even crawled
The road before me

Fearless I rode the rollercoaster of cancer
Climbing the hills of hell

Sliding, Swerving and shifting through the twists and turns
Of the ever-changing treatments and side effects
Dropping down the freefall of diagnosed death

Fearfully I staggered into the unknown
Encompassing fear
dragging, falling, and even paralyzed
On the hated road beneath me

Fearfully I laid frozen in bed
Not eating
Not working
Not living

Widower

Forever Nightmare

I feel like I'm living someone else's life
I had my life
But like a cancer
Death took it away

Now I walk the nightmare
Waiting, begging to wake up
Only to see my eyes wide open

Familiar things now foreign
People I once knew now unknowable
Places I've explored now uninspired

Like a zombie
I walk through the fog
I crawl through the sludge
Of this new life
That feels like death

Ah, death

Truly the only way out of this hell I'm in

Oh, how I wish you were here
I miss you
The kids miss you
I miss you
beyond
my worst nightmare ever was
or will be

I'm numb from the pain
I'm hurt from the numbness

Hell has no wrath
Like my woman's death
Who was loved
But is now gone

Forever

Forever in her death
Forever in this dream
Forever in this nightmare

This life of hell
That is not mine
That is now mine

Forever

Home

Swirling through my mind
You
Consuming my heart
You
Driving my actions
You

Sitting outside

Crystal blue water
Birds of paradise
Palm trees
Plumerias
Hedge

The home we created
The home you passed in
The home I dwell alone in

Swirling through my mind
?
Consuming my heart
?
Driving my actions
?

Somewhere

What a bittersweet year
Feels more bitter than sweet
The sweet is there
...somewhere

Mourning the loss of too many this year
My heart hurts and rejoices for you and your families
Shining light in a dark time

Somewhere...there's sweet smiles, joyful jollies, peaceful presence
Somewhere...there's glorious goodies, musical melodies, full families

But not here...not today

Somewhere...there's heavy hearts, soulful sorrow, empty emotions
Somewhere...there's painful past, tearful tots, deafening death

I bitterly mourn my dear sweet wife Laurie
May you rest in the arms of our Lord God and Savior Christ Jesus

Somewhere there's bitter
Somewhere there's sweet

Here there's bittersweet

XII
MONTH
LIVE LIKE
Laurie

Prayer

In the midst of
their
storm

meet them where
they are
it is
their road

walk with them

sit with them
next to them

listen
hear
validate

cry with them
hold them

In the midst of
their
emotions

Fear
Anxiety
Anger
Sadness
Regret
Guilt
Depression

be their light of hope
be their hope of healing
be their healing of life

From A to Z

The chaotic web that feels like a rat's nest
only to be unwittingly unraveled
by the One that allowed the intertwining
of the unknowns
to create
the beautifully fractured

To have the faith
to not just believe
but also to feel the belief

To experience the falling and failing of my
anxiety, fear, and panic
as the purifying fire
melts their claws away
like the - funeral pyre

The blessed faith God had
in creating our
linear left
feeling right

While our doubt lies between and lies
Whispering hints
hissing screams
lies and more lies

Eyes to see
Ears to hear
Open like flood gates
as faith washes over

The left
The right
The A
The Z

The in-between

Secret Language Lost

Lost is the kangaroo
No more chasing

Deaf are her eyes
Silent are they

Wide-eyed wonder
Shut forever

AHAW
Now ADAW

Chop chop
Chopped

Oceans to ashes

Hell, hail
Actually, gone

Friendly Phrases
Unfriended

Five shards
Fractured

Inside jokes

On the outside
Tattooed inside

Lo Siento

There's
so many things
So many days
so many words

regret...

From the earliest encounters
to the last moments
how many
holidays
birthdays
anniversaries

days...

Fight after fight
angry words
twisted words
silent words
what a waste

why...

Looking back through
tears and years

cracked...

Broken hearts
broken dreams

broken...

Tear after tear
year after year

shattered...

Wishing I would have loved you
the way you needed
the way you deserved
what was meant to be

AHAW...

A Year Ago

I said goodbye
Kissing your forehead
For the last time

Knowing you would not
Make it through the night
Only hours remained
Then only minutes

I love you
I release you into our
Father's arms

And then
Lungs settling in for...

One last breath
One last in
One last out
And then final rest

No more rage
No more fight

No more rage against the dying of the light
Go gentle, go gentle into your last goodnight

Well done, good and faithful servant

MY TODAY AND TOMORROW

EPILOGUE

Profile

I want
to love
be loved
be in love
again

I'm looking for that woman
who is willing to pour into me
as much as I pour into her

I want to feel her fingers interlaced in mine
to feel her hug from behind (just because)
that last forever
her kiss that sends shivers and tingles
through and through

I want to laugh, cry, cuddle
tell dumb jokes
listen to and hear
her heart
her tears
her unspoken

I want to have that secret language that only she and I know

I want to be silly and goofy (because I am)
but also serious and direct (because I am)

I want her to be exactly what and who she is
accepting her for all that she is and brings

I want to hear her voice each day
be excited to wake up to her
come home to her
live life with her
each
day, week, month, year...

until death does part us.

And
I want all this reciprocated

Does she exist?

Unspoken Words

The unspoken words
As I stare into your eyes

Letting go of her
While taking hold of you

The Beginning

Days, weeks, months,
Nearly a year
Has gone by

I waited patiently
Not so patiently
I waited
Consumed by tears
Surrounded by fears
Dreading the years

Grieving grief
Like never before
Like never wanted

Days, weeks, months,
Nearly a year
Has gone by

Stepping out of
Nowhere
Somewhere
Organically appearing

God-ordained

An awkward hug

Letters connecting to words
Words connecting to phrases
Phrases connecting to
Sentences to paragraphs to stories

Stories connected to smiles
Smiles connected to a second
A second connected to questions
To a third
To a kiss

INTRODUCING[15]

She loves me
She loves the kids
She loves God
She loves our family

She loves me

Tender with an edge
Edgy tenderness

Mother and wife

Eyes that shine
Smile that invites a smile

Emotions feelings
Deep thoughts

Beauty
Inside and out

Feeling all the feels

---

15 I wrote this as if I were introducing Kara to Laurie. I kept thinking about what I would say to Laurie about Kara. Laurie knew that I wanted and would most likely remarry at some point after her passing. Her one request was that whoever I married loved me, the kids, and God.

I Miss My Wife

How are you not here
How am I sitting in an airport
Alone
By myself
Without you

I dropped our daughter off for college again
And again
You weren't there

Still shaking my head in disbelief
Still wondering how this happened

Still expecting

To see your face
To hear your voice

Still

I look over and see
A random mom
Struggling with her kids
As they climb over and under chairs

Diaper bag full
Kids energy full
Mom depleted

But happy

She counts
1 – 2 – child's name
3 – child runs to her

I find myself counting

1, 2, 3, 4, 5
Little shards
(not so little any longer)
Then counting the years
30-some

Smiles of joy and tears of sadness
Swirl together
As I count your loss
2½ going on
A lifetime

Counting my blessings
Counting my loss
Counting my blessing

Counting by myself

How many passersby
Know this pain
Know this joy
Know this confusion

I miss my wife

And, I miss my wife

The guilt of missing you
The joy of loving her

The peace and abundance
The blessing she is
The one flesh we are
Hearts and lives filled

And here I sit

Feeling loved
Through your loss

I'm sorry
I'm thankful
I'm happy
I'm sad
I'm confused
I'm blessed
I'm loved

I'm sitting in the Denver Airport
By myself

Soon

Soon, I will be in my wife's arms

Acknowledgments

God
Without my Father God, none of this would be possible. I went round and round and toe-to-toe with You for several months. I've never been that angry with You before. It hurt my heart to feel so distant from You, but I thank You for allowing me the freedom to work out my feelings, especially my anger, with You and not be judged or condemned by You. I knew You would win in the end, and I wanted just that, but needed the freedom to be human and fight. Thank You for loving me enough to allow me, to be me. Thank You for bringing me through.

My Five Shards
I love you more than words can ever express. Losing mom at such a young age just sucks and is not fair. My heart hurts with and for you as you go through your own grieving process. I pray God will pick up the multitude of pieces I dropped along the way as I was stuck in my own darkness of grief. I pray that I may be the dad you need throughout your life. I am proud of you and will always love you. My five little monkeys. My five shards. My five beautiful children.

Jim & Sue LePere
I cannot fathom the grief you have endured all these years. From first hearing Laurie's diagnosis to her 9½ year battle with cancer to her watching her final days then experiencing the end. As a parent, I have no box for this. To say, "I am sorry," seems to minimize my regret, and both our sorrows. And yet, I want to say "I am sorry" every time I see you and a billion times more. Thank you for raising Laurie to be the Godly woman she was. Thank you for allowing me to love your daughter for thirty-some years and beyond. Please know my love for you knows no bounds and I am proud to be your son-in-law.

Jeff LePere
Your sister loved you so much. You held a special place in her heart, and she talked about you often. She always wanted the best for you and to see you happy.

I know she would be proud of the man you are today. Thank you for listening and supporting me in the way I needed on her last day. I will never forget.

AIMEE GUSTAFSON

You were only ten years old when Laurie and I started dating. Our bond was quickly built through laughter as your mom scolded me for teasing you as you pulled my leg hair. Not much has changed. Anyone around us could see the special relationship that you, Laurie, and I had together. Call it "three peas in a pod" or "the Mark, Laurie, Aimee Show," we three shared a lifetime of memories that will never fade.

You were Laurie's best friend and she adored you! Together, you were "sistas" and always will be.

ELLEANA GUSTAFSON

Your birthday is your birthday and Aunt Lu's death date. A bittersweet day that may be a blessing or curse. Humbly, your birthday will never be a curse or bitter. Your birthday, your birth—*you*—will always be a blessing. While you may mourn Aunt Lu this day, please do not let this overshadow the beauty of your birthday or you. This day may have fractured, but God's healing hand will bless this day, and Aunt Lu would want you to celebrate!

EMMANUEL FAITH COMMUNITY CHURCH

The support you gave our family for ten plus years blows me away. Watching the Hand of God move through His church was, and is, humbling and inspiring. I praise Christ Jesus for allowing us to be at such a loving church that supports in real time and in real ways.

RESOUNDING PRAISE HANDBELL CHOIR

Thank you for embracing Laurie and loving her. Playing handbells was truly a blessing for her, and she looked forward to each weekly practice and performance. What a blessing it was to have you play for Laurie on her last day, in her last hours of life. The fact that you came to our home, set up in our backyard, and played as the wind blew, blessed Laurie and our whole family. We cried. We smiled. We cried more.

CLASSICAL ACADEMY ADMINISTRATION, TEACHERS, STAFF, PARENTS

I cannot total the blessings you bestowed upon Laurie and our family. The countless hours given to her by loving hearts and lives. There is not enough gratitude for the over-and-beyond care you gave to Laurie and our kids as they struggled to get through each school year.

Who does this?

You did.

Our family is honored by you.

FAMILY FOCUS CHRISTIAN COUNSELING

Such leadership, by its leaders and staff, must be recognized. With the brokenness I had, even as I was blinded by the depth of my own denial, you lifted me up and carried me, even as I dragged my heals. Your support will never go unforgotten. I have many regrets regarding how broken and in denial I was and how I hid that from you. I am sorry for the damage I caused, and the trust I broke. I pray you are all blessed for the time and kindness you gave me during that dark time.

Special Thanks

Tiffany & Sharon
Thank you both again for helping my dream come true. Thank you for seeing, cultivating, and completing my vision.

Jen & Kolleen
I could think of no better Beta Readers for this book than you two. You knew Laurie and our relationship on such a deep level. Thank you for your honest input and encouragement. I will forever miss hearing the three of you playing handbells.

Kara
Only seven months after Laurie's passing, we met. I was not expecting to fall in love so soon, so quickly, so deeply. And yet, the unspoken "yes" flooded us to feeling all the feels. You held me as I cried over my deceased wife long before you became my wife. You are still holding me. Like the banks of the river, you whisper, "I got you." You are my banks and I am yours. Thank you for loving me the way you do and allowing me to finish this book. You are my wow, my indeed, my yes, and my unspoken!

From the Author

Grief is the last thing any of us wants to explore or dive deep into. Thank you, reader, for doing just that with me. The last five years have been the most difficult and confusing years in my life. Even though the doctors were clear, there was no cure for Metastatic Breast Cancer, and I was going to lose my wife, I could not comprehend what the end or the aftermath was going to be like. I found myself repeating one phrase over and over again.

"This is just weird."

I could not explain the depth or array of feelings other than through poetry.

I've thought much about what I want readers to gain from this book.

First and foremost, allow yourself to grieve in the manner you need to grieve. There's too many "shoulds" and "should nots" out there regarding grief.

Just grieve.

Yes, it hurts like hell. The pain can be beyond what we can imagine but allowing it also brings us acceptance and the ability to move forward in life.

Still, I'll admit, I don't like the word acceptance. I fight against it, even now, after five years and being remarried for three. There are still days where it does not make sense. AND that is okay!

Second, *allow for confusion.* The stages of grief are not constant or a straight line. They often move like the wind, whether it's a gentle breeze or a swirling violent tornado.

Third, let go of toxic guilt or judgment as soon as you can.

Fourth, allow yourself to move forward when you are ready. This timeline is for you and dictated by you, no one else but you.

Fifth, don't try and rush it or push through it. Grief has its own timeline.

Lastly, give yourself (and others around you) grace. You're all going to need it.

Okay, one more thing...

Most people don't know what to say or do when someone around them is grieving and will often say or do the wrong thing. Remember, they mean well. They just don't know or fully understand where you are in your grieving process.

For many people, the phrases, "they're in a better place," "you'll be okay," "God is sovereign," or "you'll see them again," are the only thing they know to say. While these may be true and helpful for some, others may find these phrases dismissive of the very real pain they are going through.

Be careful. Give grace. Try not to judge. Let people know what you need or don't need. Give more grace.

FAVORITE QUOTES TOLD TO ME:

The grief may always be with you, but it will get less paralyzing...
PASTOR DAVE

You have to find the new you, without Laurie...
EMILY, LMFT

One day, maybe sooner than you think or want, you'll have new opportunities...
JONI, LMFT

Resources

There may be times when the subject matter or poem may trigger the pain of a memory or emotional wound. You are not alone. If you need help, or someone to talk to, here are some resources to reach out to:

National Resource Center (Parenting/Relationships):
800-367-6724

National Suicide Prevention Lifeline Available 24/7 at
1-800-273-8255

You can also reach out for help by texting the word HOME to **741741**

Parents Helping Parents (free self-help support groups):
800-882-1250

Also by Mark Triboulet

Fractured Mirror Beautifully Imperfect: Poems and Prose

Coming in 2027

Fractured Moments: Mirrors of Beauty

Also by Speak Fire Publishing CEO, Tiffany Vakilian

Ugly Drawers, Pretty Panties: A Collection of Poetry, Prose, Dreams and Missives

I Need to Stay Faithful, Else Y'all Gonna F.A.A.F.O.

The Cry: Poems of Mourning Sickness

5-Day Trauma Writing Toolkit

www.ingramcontent.com/pod-product-compliance
Ingram Content Group UK Ltd.
Pitfield, Milton Keynes, MK11 3LW, UK
UKHW062311290726
14090UKWH00018B/1000